Are You The
KING
Or
QUEEN
Of Your
CASTLE?

Are You The
KING
Or
QUEEN
Of Your
CASTLE?

(Not If You Live In A Homeowner's Association)

BARRY A. ROSS

INDIE BOOKS
INTERNATIONAL

Are You The KING Or QUEEN Of Your CASTLE?

(Not If You Live In A Homeowner's Association)

No part of this publication may be reproduced or distributed in any form or by any means, without the prior permission of the publisher. Requests for permission should be directed to permissions@indiebooksintl.com, or mailed to Permissions, Indie Books International, 2511 Woodlands Way, Oceanside, CA 92054.

The views and opinions in this book are those of the author at the time of writing this book, and do not reflect the opinions of Indie Books International or its editors.

Neither the publisher nor the author is engaged in rendering legal or other professional services through this book. If expert assistance is required, the services of appropriate professionals should be sought. The publisher and the author shall have neither liability nor responsibility to any person or entity with respect to any loss or damage caused directly or indirectly by the information in this publication.

The Real Housewives is a registered trademark of Bravo Media LLC.

Disneyland is a registered trademark of Disney Enterprises, Inc.

Toontown is a registered trademark of Disney Enterprises, Inc.

ISBN-13: 978-1-957651-46-0

Library of Congress Control Number: 2023914228

Designed by Melissa@backporchcreative.com

INDIE BOOKS INTERNATIONAL®, INC.
2511 WOODLANDS WAY
OCEANSIDE, CA 92054

www.indiebooksintl.com

INDIE BOOKS
INTERNATIONAL

CONTENTS

Preface

This book aims to educate people about some of the major pitfalls in a community association based on the cases I handled in my professional law practice for fifty years. Although this book is written primarily for non-attorneys, particularly persons who own or reside in community associations (more than 30 percent of the housing in California) or are contemplating doing so, community association managers, and real estate agents, this book may also benefit attorneys who do not practice in the area of community association law.

All the stories in this book are true. However, I have changed the parties' and associations' names and the properties' locations to protect the privacy of the clients. The only exceptions are Chapters 1 and 2, where I write stories about my family. Chapter 15 is the only story that does not involve a community association. I have included this real estate case because it is interesting, educational, and demonstrates the vague line between a "win" and a "loss" in a legal dispute.

CHAPTER 1

Am I The King Of The Castle?

Approximately thirty-five years ago, my wife and I bought our first home in the Woodbridge Village Association in Irvine, California. This was our first home in a community association. At the time, we had two daughters who were two and three years old.

Upon moving into our new home, my wife and I expected to receive a cheerful greeting, perhaps a welcome basket of pastries, from the association. There was no cheerful greeting or welcome basket. Instead, we received a violation notice. Here is the background.

My wife and I noticed that our new home had a very small backyard but a large side yard. The problem is that there was a wooden fence separating the backyard from the side yard; it extended from the rear of the house to the association's common wall, thereby limiting the enclosed play area for the children to just the small backyard.

My wife and I wanted to move this wooden fence from the rear of the house to the front of the house, so that our children could play securely in both the backyard and side yard, without any concern for them going into the street in front of our house or wandering off the property. Based on this objective and after reading the association's declaration of covenants, conditions, and restrictions (CC&Rs), architectural guidelines, and the other governing documents, I prepared and submitted to the association an architectural application to move the rear wooden fence from the back of the house to the front.

I was pleasantly surprised when I was informed that the association approved my application. I then hired a contractor to demolish the existing wood fence at the rear of the house, and the contractor asked me to select a color to paint the newly installed wood fence. Since wood is brown, I chose the color brown and the contractor painted the new fence brown.

Two days later, there was a knock at the front door. It was the association's architectural compliance officer. There was no welcome basket in his hand. Rather, he had a violation notice that he handed to me for painting the fence the "wrong" color. Apparently, I made two mistakes regarding the paint color. First, I should have specified the color I wanted for the fence on my architectural application. Second, the fine print of the association's architectural guidelines stated that a fence must be painted the color of either the stucco or the trim of the house.

The stucco was gray, and the trim was green. Therefore, I had to repaint the wood fence, either gray or green. Brown was an unacceptable color.

As a real estate litigation attorney, my first instinct was to challenge the association in court over the color of my wood fence. It was my house. Wasn't I the "king of the castle"? Further, I felt the brown fence was more attractive than a green or gray fence.

As I was planning my anticipated case against the association in my head, I discussed the issue with my wife. She then looked at the brown fence and decided that the association was correct. She felt that a green or gray fence would be more attractive and requested that I repaint the fence.

Since I did not want to fight with *both* my wife and the association over the color of the fence, I went to the paint store, bought a can of gray paint, and repainted the fence. The association approved the gray color. The violation notice was withdrawn.

There is a lesson here. I am not the king of the castle. The association is the king. My wife is the queen. I am either a jack or something less than a jack.

CHAPTER 2

Can A New Career Be Launched Based On A Fleet Of Broken Boats?

Approximately thirty years ago, my daughter Michelle, then ten years old, asked me to join her for a sailboating lesson on the lake adjacent to our house. The Woodbridge Village Association offered the lesson, which required an adult to accompany minors. Since I thought this would be an enjoyable father-daughter event, I agreed to Michelle's request. I then made a reservation for the one-hour sailboating lesson on the following Saturday from 10:00 a.m. to 11:00 a.m.

When Michelle and I appeared at the dock of the lake for the sailboating lesson, I noticed five other pairs of children and adults who had also signed up for the lesson. I also saw six sailboats in the water. When the association's instructor appeared, I thought the instructor would place each pair of child and adult in each boat and provide all of us with a group sailing lesson on the lake for one hour.

The instructor had bad news. He informed the group that each sailboat had broken or damaged parts. One boat had a torn sail. One boat had a broken rudder. Another boat had a small leak. Therefore, the instructor explained that he had to jerry-build one functional boat from the six boats by transferring unbroken and undamaged parts from six boats into one well-equipped boat. Instead of a one-hour group lesson, each pair had a short ten-minute lesson in the one functional boat.

When I complained to the instructor about the poor condition of the sailboats, the instructor stated that he couldn't do anything without funding from the board of directors of the association. The instructor suggested that I direct my complaint to the board. I agreed to do so. At the next monthly board meeting, I appeared and complained about the condition of the sailboats. I explained that with a nine-million-dollar annual budget, the board of directors should be able to repair or replace the broken sailboats.

The board president said, "We will look into this matter." My facial expression must have revealed that I was disappointed with this response because the board president then said: "If you don't like the way we are running the association, why don't you run for a position on the board of directors, so that you can do a better job than we do?"

I did as the president suggested. I ran for a position on the board of directors at the next annual election and won. I was now one of seven members on the board of directors, and was installed for a two-year term.

During my first term in office, I convinced the other board members to authorize payment for six new sailboats. The following year, the new sailboats arrived.

My original plan was to serve a single two-year term, obtain authorization for new sailboats, and then conclude my involvement on the board. However, I enjoyed serving on the board and implementing other improvements within the association. Therefore, I stayed on the board and was reelected by the membership for seven consecutive two-year terms. During the last four years, I was elected annually by my fellow board members to serve as president.

As an attorney, I was assigned by the board to work with the association's general counsel on all legal issues. This involvement caused me to develop an interest in community association law, which I then incorporated into my existing real estate law practice. During the past twenty years, my law practice has been devoted exclusively to community association law. Thus, my current law practice was launched by a fleet of broken boats.

CHAPTER 3

Two Dogs Or One?

Janet Robinson was a career woman aged fifty, living by herself with two little dogs, a male and a female, in a large homeowners' association in Orange County, California, called Freedom Village. It consisted of several hundred homes. The dogs are schnauzers named Nara and Jada. A photograph of the dogs given to me by Janet is shown here. Based on the photograph, Nara and Jada believe I am the "best lawyer." This is the story behind the photograph.

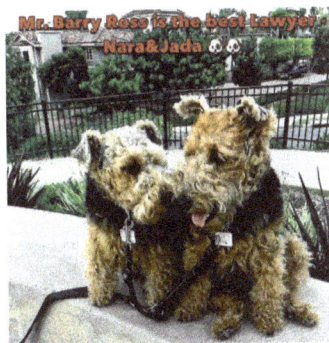

9

Janet walked her two dogs on leashes twice daily: morning and evening. During one of these walks, a representative of the association noticed the two dogs and reported this to the manager of the association. This resulted in a letter from the manager of the association to Janet informing her that the association's CC&Rs prohibited any member of the association from having more than one pet—either one dog or one cat, but not two dogs or two cats. The letter instructed Janet to remove one of her two dogs within thirty days. The association presented Janet with a *Sophie's Choice* decision: she was directed to choose which of her two dogs to give up.

Janet refused to remove either of her two dogs. The dogs were like children to her. She never had any children; she did not have a spouse or a significant other.

Janet hired me to represent her.

My challenge was to determine how to convince the association to allow Janet to keep her two dogs, when everyone else in the association is limited to one dog. I initiated two actions. First, I sent Janet to a psychologist to make an analysis and prepare a report on how the removal of one of these two dogs would affect her. The psychologist wrote a report stating that the removal of one of the two dogs would result in Janet lapsing into a depression.

Second, I sent the dogs to a class to qualify them as service animals for persons suffering from depression. The dogs are cute, but not very smart. The dogs had to take the same class twice to pass. The dogs finally passed the class. Janet received two certificates of completion.

I then sent the psychologist's report and the two certificates of completion to the association. I requested that Janet be permitted to keep both dogs, based on the federal and state fair housing laws regarding persons with disabilities, namely depression. The association reluctantly agreed to allow Janet to keep both dogs, recognizing that the association may lose in a lawsuit.

The association sent Janet a letter stating that she may keep both dogs, as long as they are well-behaved. The dogs are well-behaved and remain with Janet today. Janet showed me her appreciation by providing me with the photograph. I keep the photograph on my desk at my office, adjacent to the pictures of my children and grandchildren. When my children visited my office, they asked me why I had a photograph of these two dogs, when I didn't have any dogs of my own. I responded by explaining this case.

CHAPTER 4

Residential And Commercial Users Do Not Always Play Well Together

George Samuel was the owner of an eight-unit commercial space on the ground floor of a 220-unit residential condominium in West Los Angeles. The residential units occupied the floors above the ground floor. The name of the association was Bruin Village. The commercial space consisted of service and retail stores, such as a beauty salon, a shoe repair shop, a sandwich shop, and other similar businesses. The monthly dues were the same for the residential owners as the commercial owner, namely $400 per month.

For several years after the condominium was constructed, the residential owners and the commercial owner played nicely with each other. There were no disputes. After that, one of the residential owners must have read the CC&Rs. The association's CC&Rs, like most CC&Rs, stated that its provisions could be amended by a vote of 67 percent of the owners. Amendments could include a change in the dues structure.

Since there were 220 residential owners and only one commercial owner (comprising eight separate users), the residential owners could easily obtain a vote in excess of 67 percent to change the dues structure, which they did. The residential owners voted to increase the dues of the commercial owner by 500 percent, from $400 to $2,000 per month, while voting that there will be no increase in the dues of the residential owners.

At this point, Mr. Samuel retained my services to assist him because he felt that the 500 percent increase in his dues was unreasonable. In addition, he did not want the association to continue to raise his dues without a corresponding raise in the dues of the residential owners. I contacted the association's attorney Jeff Barnett. Mr. Barnett informed me that the association voted the dues increase properly in accordance with the CC&Rs and was not going to change its decision.

I then filed a lawsuit against the association based on the dues increase. The lawsuit was based on the fact that the majority shareholders in a corporation (namely, the association) cannot take action against the minority shareholders that benefits the majority shareholders at the expense of the minority shareholders.

One year later, at a mandatory settlement conference on the eve of the trial, we reached a settlement. The association agreed to reduce the dues increase for the commercial owner from 500 percent to 100 percent, lowering the dues from $2,000 to $800 per month. As far as I know, after the case was settled, the residential owners and the commercial owners played nicely again with each other, and there were no further increases in the dues for the commercial owner or any other disputes between the residential owners and the commercial owners.

CHAPTER 5

The Special Problem Created By Marijuana Smoke

Lisa Rice was a federal court judge in Orange County. She resided in a high-rise condominium that she had bought close to the US Courthouse in Santa Ana. The name of the association was Happy Village. Judge Rice's next-door neighbor, Jack Sander, constantly smoked marijuana and had frequent parties where marijuana was smoked. Since this was an older building that had been converted from an apartment building to condominiums, its ventilation system was very poor. The marijuana smoke from the Sander property passed directly into the Rice property, so that the Rice property continually smelled of marijuana.

You may wonder what was the problem. Marijuana smoke makes people feel happy and high. What is wrong with feeling happy and high?

The problem was that Lisa Rice was a federal court judge. As a federal court employee, she was subject to random testing for drugs and alcohol by the federal marshall. If Judge Rice was determined to have marijuana in her body, based on the random testing, she could be removed from her position as a judge. In addition, she could be criminally prosecuted. Even though California has legalized the use of marijuana, the United States government has not done so. It is still a federal crime to be under the influence of marijuana.

Judge Rice requested Mr. Sander to reduce his marijuana usage. Judge Rice also requested the association to improve the ventilation system in her condominium so that the marijuana smoke from Mr. Sander and his guests did not enter her property. Both the association and Mr. Sander ignored the requests of Judge Rice.

Judge Rice then retained me to represent her. I filed a lawsuit against Mr. Sander and the association for creating a nuisance, breaching the CC&Rs, and other claims. Mr. Sander and the association responded to the lawsuit with answers, denying the claims of Judge Rice.

Several months later, Mr. Sander sold his property to another owner who did not smoke marijuana. After Mr. Sander departed, the association claimed they had fixed the ventilation system and agreed to pay Judge Rice's attorney's fees in exchange for dismissal of the lawsuit. The lawsuit was dismissed, Judge Rice was reimbursed for her attorney's fees of $75,000, and there was no more marijuana smoke passing into Judge Rice's property.

There is one potential loose end. Since Mr. Sander vacated his property before the association "fixed" the ventilation system and the new owner of the Sander property did not smoke marijuana, I will not know for sure if the association did in fact fix the ventilation system until someone resumes smoking marijuana in the Sander property.

However, since I have not heard from Judge Rice for ten years, I believe the problem has been corrected.

CHAPTER 6

What Do You Do When Your Neighbor Harasses Your Family, But The Association Fails To Take Any Corrective Action?

John Gessel, his wife Lena Gessel, and their two minor children, Sandra, age twelve, and David, age ten, lived in a community association in Laguna Hills, California, known as the Sunset Cliffs Homeowners' Association. The association's CC&Rs contained the usual nuisance provisions, which prohibited one neighbor from being a nuisance to another neighbor in the association.

The Gessels had the neighbors from hell living three houses away from them. The neighbors George and Mary Spector, husband and wife, aged fifty and forty-eight respectively, engaged in the following activities, which the Gessels believed constituted a nuisance:

1. Mr. Spector used foul language, including "fuck you," many times in front of the Gessels and their children.

2. Mr. Spector threatened to "beat the crap" out of Mr. Gessel several times in front of Mr. Gessel's wife and children.

3. Mr. Spector yelled and cursed at the Gessel children when driving his car while the Gessel children were playing in the street in front of their house.

4. Mrs. Spector smacked Sandra Gessel on the butt. Mrs. Spector said she was just being "friendly."

5. Mr. Spector threw a glass bottle down in the street, shattering the bottle into sharp little pieces of glass adjacent to the Gessel driveway. Mr. Spector did not remove the broken glass, leaving this chore to the Gessels.

The Gessels retained me to represent them.

I contacted the association and requested that the association enforce the nuisance provision of the CC&Rs against the Spectors based on their above-described conduct. The association responded that it sent a letter to the Spectors based on the Gessels' complaints. In the letter, the association requested that the Spectors demonstrate "civility" and "respect" toward the Gessels.

However, the letter just made them Spectors behave more aggressively toward the Gessels.

When I asked the association why it did not proceed with a disciplinary hearing and the imposition of fines and penalties against the Spectors when its letter was ignored, the association responded by stating that this was a "neighbor-to-neighbor dispute" and neighbors have to work out their differences on their own, without further involvement of the association.

I contemplated filing a lawsuit against the association for its failure to enforce the nuisance provision of the CC&Rs. However, after giving this matter more thought, I decided to pursue the alternative path of filing a harassment petition against the Spectors requesting a judge to order the Spectors to stay fifty feet away from the Gessels, to refrain from any verbal or written communications with the Gessels, and, more generally, to have no further contact with them.

The harassment petition was filed and served. A date was set for the trial. There was a five-day trial in the Orange County Superior Court before Judge Roberta Sands. The Spectors were represented by counsel. Judge Sands initially expressed concerns that the Spectors' comments were protected by "freedom of speech" based on the First Amendment of the US Constitution, that Mr. Spector never actually touched Mr. Gessel, and that Mrs. Spector's touching of Mrs. Gessel was an innocent gesture. However, after hearing all the evidence, including the compelling testimony of the Gessels' children, who explained how upset and terrified they were by the actions of the Spectors, Judge Sands issued the requested restraining order.

Since then, to my knowledge, there have been no further incidents between the Gessels and the Spectors. The restraining order was an effective remedy.

My decision to bypass a lawsuit against the association and proceed directly against the Spectors turned out to be the correct path to take.

CHAPTER 7

Will Toontown Colors Create An Uproar In Your Association?

While I was serving as president of the board of directors of the Woodbridge Village Association, a master-planned residential community in Irvine known for its uniformity of architectural design, landscaping, and home colors, Mr. and Mrs. Stengel submitted an architectural application to paint the exterior of their house, selecting light blue for the stucco and light green for the trim.

The architectural application included a one-square-inch color sample of each color for approval. The architectural committee reviewed the application and approved it. There was no opposition by any neighbors.

The Stengels proceeded to paint their house the approved colors. Within two to three days, the painting was completed.

The neighborhood was outraged by the colors of the house because (1) no other house in the association was painted these colors, (2) the paint colors bore a striking resemblance to the color scheme at Toontown in Disneyland, (3) the neighbors claimed the painting of the Stengel house would diminish the market value of all nearby homes, and (4) the association generally prohibits any paint colors that do not match the other paint colors on the same street and in the same neighborhood. More than one hundred property owners signed a petition or sent letters to the association complaining of the colors of the Stengels' house. Some letters threatened to recall the board of directors for the alleged travesty.

The board of directors of the association scheduled a hearing to discuss the painting of the Stengels' house. Mr. Stengel, an attorney, appeared at the hearing wearing a light blue shirt and light green slacks to emphasize the point that these colors are a reasonable combination. No one else appeared to speak in support of the colors of the Stengel house. Approximately fifty angry people appeared to oppose the colors of this house.

After the hearing, the association offered to pay to repaint the Stengel house more traditional colors, but the Stengels declined the offer.

As a result of this incident, the association changed its architectural approval process. First, the proposed colors must be painted on a wall of the house prior to approval so that persons can better experience what the colors will look like when the house is painted. This is in addition to submitting the one-square-inch sample of each color. Second, neighbor awareness (notification to neighbors of the architectural change) was extended from the next-door neighbors to other neighbors in the area.

In conclusion, the Stengel house retains the light blue/ light green color scheme. Although the board of directors was not recalled, several incumbent board members were replaced by nonincumbents at the next board election, which does not usually occur. Finally, the board of directors of the association started taking a more careful approach to the approval of paint colors. No other house in the association will be painted with Toontown colors.

CHAPTER 8

Is Filming Prohibited In A Community Association?

John Foreman wanted to produce a television show.

John resided in a gated, exclusive, and expensive community association in Orange County that consisted of more than one thousand homes, a prestigious golf course, many parks and playgrounds, and a clubhouse with a first-class dining room. The name of the association was Residential Village.

John's idea for a television show consisted of two elements: video recording interviews with neighbors and video recording neighbors interacting within their residences with their family members, as well as with other neighbors. The neighbors consented to the interviews and the video recordings. The same five or six sets of neighbors would appear in each show.

The neighbors seemed to be selected for their communication skills and their physical attractiveness. Prior to filming the neighbors, John would suggest topics for the neighbors to discuss. However, the videotaping was unscripted.

The representatives of the association noticed the arrival of film crews with trucks, lighting, and sound equipment. Also, they noticed John filming the neighbors outside their homes, walking or jogging, getting into their cars, or dining at the clubhouse. The attorney for the association, Sam Reynolds, wrote a cease and desist letter to John stating that he must stop all filming because it violated the association's rules. The letter stated that the residential CC&Rs prohibited any commercial activity in the association, and John's filming constituted commercial activity. Prohibition of commercial activity is a common provision in CC&Rs.

John hired me to represent him. I called Sam, who informed me that he had been instructed by the board of directors of the association to file a lawsuit against John to obtain an injunction to prevent John from further filming.

I explained to Sam that John was not engaged in commercial activity. Rather, John was simply interviewing and recording his neighbors, with the consent of the same neighbors, and most of the filming was inside their homes. I explained that the association did not have the authority to control what people say and do inside their homes. I further explained that John's filming was a form of free speech protected by the US Constitution.

I could tell that I was not convincing Sam to change his opinion and that we were headed toward expensive and time-consuming litigation. More significantly, any stoppage of the filming at this point would prevent John from submitting the project to a television station and leave John with all of the expense of production, but without any revenue from the production.

I asked Sam what were the primary wishes of the association. He stated: "First, the filming could not continue for a long, indefinite period of time. Second, the filming must not identify the association. Third, the filming must be limited to specified hours and days."

After considerable negotiation, Sam and I agreed on the following resolution:

1. All filming would stop in ninety days and never be resumed again thereafter.

2. The name of the association would not be mentioned or shown. Further, nothing that would identify the association would be shown in the filming. Thus, there would be no filming of the entry gate, the golf course, or the clubhouse.

3. The hours of filming would be limited from 9:00 a.m. to 5:00 p.m. Monday through Friday. There would be no filming on Saturday or Sunday.

Based on this agreement, John's filming continued and was completed within the ninety-day time period. The project was then submitted to several television networks, accepted by one such network, and then appeared on television.

The name of the show was *The Real Housewives Of Orange County*. It was very popular and successful.

The show transitioned into a series of shows including *The Real Housewives of Beverly Hills, New York City,* and most recently *Dubai.*

The show was so successful and profitable for John that he never had to work another day in his life.

If I had taken this case on a contingent fee/royalty basis, I would never have had to work another day in my life. But I was not as entrepreneurial as John. So, I continue to work.

CHAPTER 9

Does Free Speech Apply To The Election Of The Board Of Directors Of A Community Association?

There was excitement in the air on the evening of September 17, 2009. It was the night of the annual election of the board of directors of Freedom Village Homeowners' Association. The election would determine who would manage, direct, and control the association for the next year. The association is a gated community consisting of 228 condominiums in Fountain Valley.

There were two antagonists: Betsy Calder, the eventual plaintiff, and Mark Alton, the eventual defendant. Mark Alton was the current president of the association, and he wanted to be reelected to the board, along with the current board members. Betsy Calder was the immediate prior president of the association, and she wanted her slate of people to be elected to the board to replace the existing board, including Mark Alton.

Ms. Calder and Mr. Alton were both real estate agents, who worked in the same real estate office and competed with each other for listings and sales within the association. Ms. Calder and Mr. Alton disliked each other.

Approximately seventy-five people were present at the meeting for the election of the board of directors. Mr. Alton called the meeting to order. Mr. Alton then invited persons present to speak. Ms. Calder went to the podium. She stated that Mr. Alton and the current board had mismanaged the association's finances and that they should not be reelected to the board. She stated that her recommended group of people would do a much better job.

When Ms. Calder had completed her comments, Mr. Alton did not immediately call for the next speaker. If he had, the story would probably end here and there would have been no subsequent court case.

Instead, Mr. Alton responded to the comments of Ms. Calder. He stated that there had been no financial mismanagement by the current board of directors and that these statements were untrue. Further, Mr. Alton stated that Ms. Calder had stolen $100 from the association when she was president. He explained that she had purchased a three-in-one fax, copier, scanner machine from Staples for the association with an association credit card. As part of the purchase, Ms. Calder had received a rebate of $100 from Staples that was sent to her home address and had never delivered it to the association. He then proceeded to place blown-up images of the purchase, the rebate coupon, and the rebate check on the wall behind the board of directors, so that all persons present could see the documentary evidence of the $100 rebate. Then Mr. Alton called for the next speaker.

Following presentations by numerous speakers, persons present cast their ballots for the board of directors. The current board, including Mr. Alton, was reelected.

Several days later, Ms. Calder filed a lawsuit against Mr. Alton and the association in the Orange County Superior Court for defamation. She stated Mr. Alton lied when he called her a thief at the board meeting. I was retained to represent Mr. Alton and the association.

After reviewing the lawsuit, I made a motion to dismiss the case based on the SLAPP statute, which stands for Strategic Lawsuit Against Public Participation. The SLAPP statute states that if a person is sued for exercising his or her constitutional First Amendment right to freedom of speech the lawsuit should be dismissed by the judge. The rationale is that no one should be sued for exercising their constitutionally protected freedom of speech. I asserted that Mr. Alton was exercising his freedom of speech when he stated that Ms. Calder was a thief.

At the hearing in the Orange County Superior Court, Judge Janice Montgomery ruled that the SLAPP statute did not apply and denied my motion to dismiss the case. I believed that her decision was incorrect. I therefore appealed Judge Montgomery's decision to the California Court of Appeal. Two years later, the Court of Appeal agreed with me, holding that Judge Montgomery was wrong, the case should be dismissed, and Mr. Alton and the association were entitled to recover their attorneys' fees from Ms. Calder.

There were two results. First, this case is established case law in California and can be referenced as binding precedent. Second, I have had to decline to accept cases from prospective new clients where the clients wanted me to sue their associations because board members called them bad names, such as thief, crook, fraud, etc., based on the holding of this case.

CHAPTER 10

A Dog-Poop Problem Metastasizes

There were two adjacent owner-occupied units in an upscale residential community association in Ventura, known as Happy Acres. My client, Sam Jones, did not have any pets. His neighbor, Mike Pearse, had a German shepherd dog named Spike.

Every morning, Mr. Pearse took Spike for a walk. The walk began with Spike depositing his poop on the pristine front lawn of Mr. Jones. Although Mr. Pearse would have a doggy bag with him, he would not use it to remove the dog poop. Instead, Mr. Pearse would continue walking with Spike.

Mr. Jones observed this daily routine by Mr. Pearse and Spike and one day asked Mr. Pearse, "Why don't you pick up after your dog?"

Mr. Pearse responded by stating, "Fuck you."

Mr. Jones then picked up Spike's poop in a doggie bag and proceeded to the office of the association's community manager, Stella Reamer. Mr. Jones relayed the pertinent information to Ms. Reamer, including showing her the contents of the doggie bag. Mr. Jones stated, "I want the association to take disciplinary action against Mr. Pearse based on his failure to remove Spike's poop from my lawn."

Ms. Reamer replied, "The association will not initiate any disciplinary action against Mr. Pearse until you provide a photograph or a videotape of Spike pooping on your lawn and Mr. Pearse failing to retrieve the poop."

Frustrated, but determined, Mr. Jones then proceeded to Costco to purchase a video camera motion detector. After purchasing the camera, Mr. Jones installed it on the inside of the glass window in his house adjacent to his front door. The camera was installed on the inside of the house, but it could be seen from the outside of the house.

The camera worked perfectly. Whenever any person or animal passed in front of the Jones residence, the camera was activated and began filming. Upon the persons or animals departing from the front of the Jones residence, the camera stopped filming.

The next morning, Mr. Pearse began his morning walk with Spike. He noticed the camera in the front window of the Jones residence. He did not stop on Mr. Jones' front lawn but continued walking Spike past his house. No poop was deposited on the front lawn of the Jones residence.

Mr. Jones was pleased. He believed he had solved the problem with his neighbor. This story would have ended at this point, but for the intervention of the association.

About one week later, Mr. Jones received a cease and desist letter from the association community manager, Ms. Reamer. Ms. Reamer stated in her letter: "The camera must be removed because it is not permitted in the association. The camera invades the privacy of the association's members by recording them in the common area without their knowledge or consent."

Mr. Jones decided to ignore the letter from Ms. Reamer because he was not going to remove the camera.

About one month later, Mr. Jones received a fine notice for $100 from Ms. Reamer because he had not removed the camera. Mr. Jones ignored the fine notice because he was not going to remove the camera or pay the fine.

Every month thereafter, Ms. Reamer sent Mr. Jones another fine notice. But each such notice doubled the fine from the previous month. In the second month, the fine was $200. In the third month the fine was $400. After several additional months, the fines exceeded $5,000, which constituted a lien on the Jones property. The fines would have to be paid when Mr. Jones sold or refinanced his property.

At this point, Mr. Jones hired me to assist him.

I filed a lawsuit against the association seeking to cancel the fines because the association had no authority to regulate the activity of Mr. Jones inside his house. The CC&Rs stated that the association had authority to approve any changes Mr. Jones made to the "exterior" of the residence but had no such authority to approve any changes to the "interior" of the residence. The camera was inside rather than outside. Further, the CC&Rs did not prohibit or even mention cameras. The association's attorney contended that the *effect* of the camera was outside the house and invaded the privacy of the association's members.

A judge in Ventura ruled in favor of Mr. Jones. He said that the association had no authority to fine Mr. Jones for a camera installed inside the house, even though the filming was outside the house. Further, the judge ruled that members have no expectation of privacy while walking on the exterior pathways and sidewalks of the association. The judge canceled all the fines. The judge stated that if the association wanted to regulate cameras, it must formally adopt such a rule after the members have notice and an opportunity to be heard on the rule before it is adopted. Finally, the judge awarded attorney's fees to Mr. Jones in the amount of $3,000.

Mr. Jones's camera remains inside his house by his front door and Spike no longer leaves poop on his front lawn.

CHAPTER 11

RV—To Be Or Not To Be

My client Sam Ward was a single man, retired from his position as an executive with Pepsi. Sam decided that for his retirement he would buy a recreational vehicle and take vacations around the United States. Sam bought a new recreational vehicle and parked it in front of his residence. Sam lived in a community association in Fountain Valley named Freedom Trail. A few days after Sam bought the recreational vehicle, he encountered the association president, Virginia Bane, on the street of the association. Virginia told him: "Recreational vehicles are not permitted in our association, based on our governing documents. You will have to park the recreational vehicle outside the association in a storage facility." Sam responded by stating: "I am not going to move my recreational vehicle from the front of my house. You can't make me do so."

Virginia conferred with association attorney Janet Pano and requested her to initiate a lawsuit against Sam to require him to relocate his recreational vehicle outside the association. Janet did as requested and filed the lawsuit.

Sam then retained me to represent him. I reviewed the lawsuit and the association's CC&Rs. The CC&Rs stated in clear language that no one in the association may maintain a recreational vehicle anywhere in the association. All recreational vehicles must be stored outside the association. There were no exceptions to this rule. Based on my knowledge of established case law, I knew that this rule prohibiting recreational vehicles was enforceable in a community association.

I recommended to Sam that he relocate his recreational vehicle outside the association in a storage facility and that I would attempt to negotiate a settlement with the association's attorney whereby the lawsuit against Sam would be dismissed with Sam paying the association no attorney's fees or costs. I explained to Sam that if he proceeded to trial, he would lose the case in the Orange County Superior Court, which would result in the requirement that he relocate his recreational vehicle outside the association. In addition, I explained that he would then be required to pay the association's attorney's fees and court costs, which I estimated would be approximately $100,000.

I expected Sam to follow my recommendation. Instead, he rejected my recommendation. He stated: "I have researched you, Mr. Ross. You win most of your cases against community associations. You will win this case. You are a very good lawyer. I am willing to take my chances on you and this case."

I responded: "I may be a good lawyer, but I am not a magician. I cannot make the words in the CC&Rs change or go away. The words in the CC&Rs clearly prohibit any recreational vehicle in the association."

After further discussion, I realized that Sam was not going to change his mind no matter what I said. I took the case, realizing that I would probably lose the case and disappoint Sam.

I then reviewed the association's rules for initiating disciplinary matters against members who violate the CC&Rs. The rules stated that the following process must be initiated by the association before it may file a lawsuit against a member for violating the CC&Rs:

1. First, the association must send a letter to the owner stating the nature of the violation and requesting the owner to stop the violation within ten days after the date of the letter.

2. Second, if the violation continues beyond the ten-day time period, the association must send the owner a second letter inviting the owner to a hearing before

the board of directors to determine if the alleged violation had occurred and what the punishment should be—fines, loss of privileges, lawsuit, etc.

3. Third, the board of directors must conduct a hearing where the owner may present his defense to the association.

4. Fourth, the board must find the owner in violation of a specific provision of the CC&Rs.

5. Fifth, the association must send a third letter to the owner notifying him of the decision and the reasons for the decision.

The association did none of these five items.

At trial before Judge Henry Smith of the Orange County Superior Court, I presented the defense that the association failed to follow its own rules, namely one through five above, for disciplining a member before initiating a lawsuit against a member for a violation of the CC&Rs.

At the conclusion of the trial, Judge Smith agreed with me, ruling in favor of Sam because the association failed to follow its own rules. Judge Smith dismissed the association's lawsuit.

Since Sam was the prevailing party, Judge Smith also ordered the association to reimburse Sam for his attorney's fees and costs in the amount of $90,000, based on my hourly rate of $400.

About two weeks later, I received a check from the association for $90,000, which I then forwarded to Sam because Sam had initially paid my attorney's fees and costs.

As far as I know, Sam's recreational vehicle is still in front of his residence.

CHAPTER 12

The Most Expensive Dividing Wall Between Residences

Mr. and Mrs. Kay owned and occupied a single-family residence in a community association in Dana Point overlooking Dana Point Harbor known as Ocean View Estates.

Within the association, each residence was originally constructed as a single-story home and was surrounded by a six-foot-high cement wall in order to protect the privacy of the property owners. As originally constructed, the residences did not have any views of Dana Point Harbor, but they did have very private backyards.

The Kays had a swimming pool in their backyard. Each morning, the Kays' morning exercise consisted of swimming laps in the nude. This continued for many years without any problems.

During recent times, several property owners within the association wanted to add second stories to their homes because their families grew and they needed more space, and/or they wanted a view of Dana Point Harbor from a new second-story addition.

In most cases, the association approved second-story additions, despite complaints from neighbors that they invaded their privacy, since the windows of the new second stories looked directly into the backyards and windows of the neighbors' houses.

Mr. and Mrs. Kay's next-door neighbor, Dr. Denise Login, a single woman, submitted an application to the association to construct a second-story addition. The Kays objected to the second-story addition based on an invasion of privacy. Article 1 of the California Constitution states that all persons have certain "inalienable rights" including "privacy." The association rejected the privacy objection by the Kays and authorized Dr. Login to proceed with the second-story addition.

The Kays did not have a strong case until Dr. Login became greedy. If Dr. Login had constructed her second story in accordance with the association approved plans, there probably would not have been any lawsuit filed. However, Dr. Login decided to add more windows and larger windows to maximize her view of Dana Point Harbor.

These had not been depicted on the approved plans for her second-story addition. Once the addition was constructed, the Kays noticed that Dr. Login's windows did not comply with the approved plans and notified the association of this noncompliance. The association, however, took no corrective action against Dr. Login.

At this point, the Kays retained me to represent them. I filed a lawsuit on behalf of the Kays against Dr. Login and the association. The association filed a cross-complaint against Dr. Login for noncompliance with the approved plans.

The lawsuit dragged on for more than one year without any resolution. Finally, on the eve of the trial, the parties agreed to participate in nonbinding mediation before retired Judge Robert Prince. After three day-long mediation sessions, Judge Prince negotiated a resolution of the lawsuit that was acceptable to all parties. The lawsuit would be dismissed, with each party paying their own attorney's fees and costs. A twelve-foot slanted wall at the edge of the Kay property adjacent to the Login property would be constructed. The wall resembled the Leaning Tower of Pisa. The slanted wall on the Kay property allowed Dr. Login to see Dana Point Harbor from her second-story windows, but prevented Dr. Login from seeing any portion of the Kays' backyard or swimming pool.

The new wall looked like this:

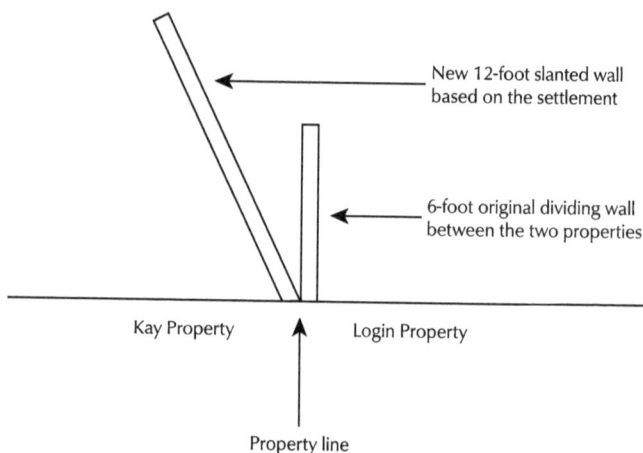

New 12-foot slanted wall based on the settlement

6-foot original dividing wall between the two properties

Kay Property

Login Property

Property line

The cost of engineering and constructing the new twelve-foot wall on the Kay property was paid for by the association. No other money exchanged hands, even though each party had spent more than $100,000 on attorney's fees.

After spending a cumulative total of more than $300,000 on attorney's fees and several thousand dollars for the new wall, the case was settled. Considering the attorney's fees spent, this was probably the most expensive wall ever constructed between residences.

The Kays continue to swim nude in their swimming pool. Dr. Login has a great view of Dana Point Harbor. All is now peaceful among the Kays, Dr. Login, and the association.

CHAPTER 13

You Must Never Lie To Your Attorney

Jason and Joanne McManis, husband and wife, resided in a single-family residence in a high-end homeowners' association in Orange County known as Heavenly Hills, with their son John, age fourteen, an aspiring basketball player about to enter high school. Mr. and Mrs. McManis thought that with proper training, their son could develop into a professional basketball player.

Mr. and Mrs. McManis had a large backyard. The backyard was decorated with attractive landscaping and a half-court basketball court, where son John practiced and received basketball lessons.

Mr. and Mrs. McManis decided to remodel their backyard to provide more attractive landscaping and a full-court basketball court for John.

Mr. and Mrs. McManis submitted an architectural application to the association. The application was approved by the association. Mr. and Mrs. McManis proceeded to reconstruct their backyard in accordance with the approved plans.

The association had extensive horse trails and a community horse track for horse racing and horse contests. Many of the owners within the association stabled horses in their backyards. It seemed like there were two types of people in the association: horse lovers and horse haters.

The horse lovers liked the horse trails and the community horse track. They wanted the horse trails and the community horse track to remain in pristine condition and did not care how much association money was spent to do so. The horse lovers did not want other property owners to install basketball courts, tennis courts, or any other features that made noise that might "spook" the horses as they galloped in the association common area trails immediately behind the residences. The horse haters disliked all the spending of association funds for the benefit of horse lovers and usually had backyards that included tennis courts or basketball courts that were hated by the horse lovers for the noises made that spooked their horses.

The control of the board of directors of the association frequently changed between horse haters and horse lovers with each subsequent election of the board.

Against this background, Mr. and Mrs. McManis obtained architectural approval when the board consisted of horse haters. But by the time Mr. and Mrs. McManis were completing their construction of the backyard, the board consisted of horse lovers.

At the conclusion of construction of the backyard, a representative of the association visited the McManis property to determine if Mr. and Mrs. McManis constructed their rear yard in accordance with the approved plans. This is a common procedure in homeowners' associations.

The representative of the association who made the site inspection noticed that the new rear property cement wall surrounding the backyard was unusually close to the common area horse trail. This led to further investigation by the association and a demand letter from the association accusing Mr. and Mrs. McManis of extending their backyard into the association's common area and demanding that they demolish and remove all of their improvements in the common area, including the newly constructed full-court basketball court. Mr. and Mrs. McManis disputed this contention, stating that they constructed the rear cement wall in the same location as the rear fence that had existed previously. There was no survey of the McManis property by either the association or Mr. and Mrs. McManis at this time.

Mr. and Mrs. McManis retained me to represent them. Mr. and Mrs. McManis assured me that the current rear cement wall was in exactly the same location as the previous iron fence that existed prior to the remodeling. I based my defense of Mr. and Mrs. McManis on their representation that the new rear wall was in the same location as the prior rear fence that had been in place for twenty years. From the information provided, I believed I had a good defense based on adverse possession/prescriptive easement and other legal theories. After an exchange of letters with the association's attorney, it was clear that there was no way to resolve this dispute and litigation ensued. The association filed a complaint against Mr. and Mrs. McManis in the Orange County Superior Court. Mr. and Mrs. McManis filed a cross-complaint against the association. There were several exchanges of interrogatories and requests to produce documents.

There were about fifteen depositions. Each party retained surveyors to conduct surveys of the McManis property. The two surveys were virtually identical. The surveys showed that the McManis backyard trespassed thirty feet into the association common area. The factual issue to determine was whether the prior rear iron fence was in the same location as the current cement wall or thirty feet closer to the McManis house than the current cement wall.

As we proceeded to trial, and more evidence and information became available, it became more and more apparent that Mr. and Mrs. McManis had lied to the association and me about the location of the prior backyard iron fence line. In short, Mr. and Mrs. McManis had knowingly constructed the new rear cement wall thirty feet into the common area from the prior rear yard iron fence, in order to have enough room to construct a full-court basketball court for their son. The case proceeded to trial before Judge Wilkes of the Orange County Superior Court. Judge Wilkes ruled in favor of the association and ordered Mr. and Mrs. McManis to demolish and remove their backyard improvements that extended beyond their property line, which was the location of the prior iron fence, and reimburse the association for all of its attorney's fees and costs.

Following the loss at trial before Judge Wilkes, Mr. and Mrs. McManis appealed their case to the California Court of Appeal, where three justices rejected the appeal, ruling in favor of the association and affirming the decision of Judge Wilkes.

The costs to Mr. and Mrs. McManis to demolish and restore their backyard to its original condition, including the removal of the basketball court, plus the association's attorney's fees exceeded $1,000,000, which the McManis's paid to the association. This case was the worst loss of my fifty-year legal career. This case was also the worst experience in the life of Mr. and Mrs. McManis. The lesson here is very simple: do not lie to your attorney.

CHAPTER 14

A Picture Is Worth
A Thousand Words

Mr. and Mrs. Jackson resided in a community association in Orange County known as Sunny Village.

The Jacksons decided to demolish and reconstruct their backyard. The Jacksons submitted an architectural application to the association. The association approved the architectural application. The Jacksons then constructed their backyard according to the approved application. If the tale ended here, there would be no story to tell; however, that is not the case.

After the Jacksons completed their backyard remodel, they decided to install "playground equipment" in the backyard. The "playground equipment" was referenced as "playground equipment" but not physically described in the architectural plans approved by the association.

The association objected to the improvements installed because they looked less like "playground equipment" and more like an "accessory structure."

The association's rules stated that any "accessory structure" must not exceed six feet in height. The "playground equipment" was eight feet high and the regulations stated that "playground equipment" may be nine feet high. The "playground equipment" couldn't be reduced in height; it would need to be either completely demolished or retained in its current condition.

The issue to be decided was whether the installation was in fact "playground equipment" or an "accessory structure." The Jacksons contended it was "playground equipment." The association contended it was an "accessory structure."

Admittedly, the installation has several uses, such as a movie theater and a diving platform. Here is where a picture is worth a thousand words. Photos #1 and #2 show the "swing set" and the movie theater controls.

Photo #1

Photo #2

Photo #3 shows the complete structure. Photo #4 shows the view from the street toward the Jackson property. It shows that the installation was obscured by the association's trees.

Photo #3

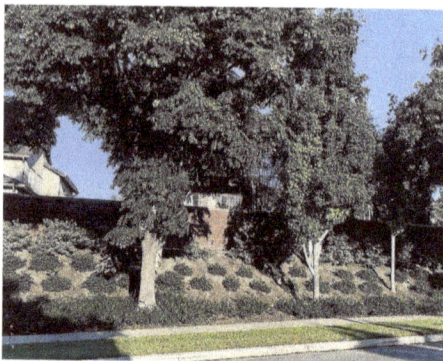

Photo #4

Was the installation "playground equipment" or an "accessory structure"? This is the issue for a judge or jury to determine at some future time. Based on the photos, how would you vote? The author believes that this will be a difficult case for the Jacksons to win.

CHAPTER 15

You Can Win The Battle, But Lose The War

In 2002, Martin Bash and Marlene Bash, husband and wife, psychologist and dentist, wanted to buy a home in the Turtle Rock area of Irvine. Their children were at the time in middle school, and the Bashes wanted a house in Turtle Rock because its local high school was University High School, which, because of its recognized academic achievement, sends its students to the best colleges in the United States.

In 2002, home prices were escalating rapidly in Southern California, and particularly in Turtle Rock. After researching homes in the area, the Bashes made several offers for homes in the price range they could afford, but each time they were outbid by others. Finally, the Bashes made an offer on a home that was accepted. The purchase price was $540,000.

The sellers were John Moore and Sarah Moore, husband and wife. The Bashes and the Moores were represented by separate real estate agents.

The Bashes were elated. But the elation did not last long. The Moores subsequently received a purchase offer from Sam Nest for $565,000. The Moores then notified the Bashes that they were not going to complete the contract with the Bashes because Mr. Nest had offered them more money for their home.

The Bashes then retained me to represent them.

I observed that the purchase contract was signed by all four parties (the Moores and the Bashes) and it appeared to be complete and enforceable.

Since I was concerned the Moores would sell their home to Sam Nest, thereby depriving the Bashes of the home, I promptly filed a civil lawsuit for specific performance (to enforce the contract) and declaratory relief against the Moores. In addition, I recorded a notice of lis pendens (pending action) in the office of the Orange County Recorder to prevent the Moores from transferring title to the property to Sam Nest or anyone else.

After the lawsuit was filed and the lis pendens was recorded, I spoke with the attorney for the Bashes, Martin Young. I asked Mr. Young what defense he was going to assert on behalf of the Moores. Mr. Young replied, "The Moores did not sign the purchase contract."

I responded by asking, "If the Moores did not sign the purchase contract, who signed their names?"

Mr. Young responded, "The Moores' real estate agent Kate Sanders of Prestige California Real Estate signed their names to the purchase contract without their authorization."

This simple case had just become much more complicated.

The Moores filed an answer to my complaint, denying that they had signed the purchase contract. The Moores also filed a cross-complaint against their real estate agent for indemnity. On behalf of the Bashes, I then filed a cross-complaint against the Moores' real estate agent for fraud.

The Moores' real estate agent admitted that she had signed the names of the Moores to the purchase contract, but she contended, "The Moores requested me to sign their names, because they did not want to lose the opportunity to sell their house to the Bashes at a good price."

This complicated set of facts resulted in two trials before the Orange County Superior Court: a trial by a judge over liability and then a trial by a jury over damages. In addition, there were four separate appeals to the California Court of Appeal, resulting in four published Court of Appeal opinions.

The conclusion of this litigation, which consumed more than five years, was as follows:

1. The Bashes became the owners of the Moore property for the contracted purchase price of $540,000. This was a good result for the Bashes because the house was worth over $1 million at the conclusion of the litigation.

2. The Moores had to pay all of the attorney's fees and costs incurred by the Bashes, in the amount of $250,000. This sum was deducted from the purchase price of $540,000, resulting in a net purchase price to the Bashes of $290,000. Also, the Court of Appeal stated that $250,000 was a fair price to pay for my services. I was happy to read this comment in the decision of the Court of Appeal, namely that my attorney's fees were "reasonable."

3. The Moores' real estate agent was dismissed from the litigation because the judge believed that the Moores had directed the agent to sign their names to the purchase contract. Shortly thereafter, the California Department of Real Estate issued an alert to the state's real estate agents stating that real estate agents must not sign their clients' names to contracts.

4. Since the litigation lasted more than five years, the Bashes' children were already in college by the time they took title to the Moores' property. None of the

children attended University High School. Although the Bashes won the battle, they did not win the war (or the original objective of the litigation) because they were not able to enroll their children in University High School.

CHAPTER 16

The Child From Hell

Mr. and Mrs. Robertson, residents of Dana Point, also owned a condominium in Orange, in a community association known as Pleasant Valley.

The Robertsons' only son, Eric Robertson, his girlfriend Bessie, and their three children under five did not have the financial resources to rent their own housing. So the Robertsons rented them their condominium in Orange. Although a rental agreement for the payment of rent was signed, Eric never paid his parents any rent.

It did not take long until Eric was involved in a dispute with the association concerning the condominium in Orange. The association complained that Eric was engaging in an automobile repair business in the garage, driveway, and the adjacent association street. In addition, Eric made threatening and abusive statements toward the association's representatives. The automobile repair business and the foul and threatening language violated the provisions of the association's CC&Rs.

When Mr. and Mrs. Robertson, as the condominium owners, received notices from the association regarding Eric's wrongful actions, they asked him to discontinue his automobile business and abusive language. Eric ignored the requests by his parents and the repeated violation notices from the association.

The association then filed a lawsuit against the Robertsons and Eric for violating the CC&Rs. I was retained to represent the Robertsons and Eric.

For reasons best known to Eric, he decided that he could do a better job representing himself than I could do. So Eric signed a substitution of attorney, stating that he was representing himself. After protracted negotiations, I was able to negotiate a settlement agreement with the association on behalf of Mr. and Mrs. Robertson. The settlement agreement required the Robertsons to sell their condominium and remove Eric from the condominium within one year. In exchange, the association agreed to waive its claim against the Robertsons for attorney's fees and costs and dismiss its lawsuit. Eric declined to participate in the settlement negotiations or the settlement agreement.

Eric refused to move out of the condominium. He refused to allow the Robertsons' real estate agent or any other real estate agent to show the condominium to prospective buyers. To make matters worse, he began to damage the interior of the condominium maliciously and intentionally.

Upon the request of the Robertsons, I initiated an unlawful detainer action in court to evict Eric, his girlfriend Bessie, and their three minor children from the condominium. Due to COVID-19 regulations and Eric's obstructions, the eviction process took several months longer than expected. But eventually Eric and his family were evicted by the Orange County marshall.

Prior to the eviction, Eric and Bessie became involved in a knife fight with their next-door neighbors inside the condominium. The knife fight included the neighboring husband and wife, Eric's girlfriend Bessie, and Eric. It was a knife fight among four people.

As a result of the knife fight, Eric and Bessie were charged by the Orange County district attorney with felony assault and battery on the neighbors. The criminal charges were eventually dismissed. However, the neighbors filed a civil lawsuit against Eric, Bessie, and the Robertsons as owners of the property. I represented Mr. and Mrs. Robertson in this case. The Robertsons' liability was based on the fact that they allowed a dangerous person to occupy their property. As of this writing, that case is still pending.

To make matters worse, after Eric was evicted, he filed a civil lawsuit against his parents for wrongful eviction and improperly settling the association lawsuit. I represented the Robertsons in that case. I caused that case to be dismissed with a pretrial motion.

Eric reported me to the State Bar of California for disciplinary action alleging wrongful actions in representing the Robertsons against him. The State Bar has taken no action against me.

This unfortunate saga never seems to end. Like cancer, it grows and becomes worse. Eric is truly the child from hell.

CHAPTER 17

My Clients Did Everything Wrong

Dr. and Mrs. Sanders owned and resided in a high-end single-family residence in Newport Beach, California, near the Pacific Ocean. The home was located within a homeowners' association known as Ocean View Terrace. Each home in the association was terraced so that the adjacent home closest to the ocean was at a lower level. This was designed to maximize ocean views from all homes.

The association's CC&Rs stated that all landscaping must be approved by the association and no landscaping may interfere with any other owners' views of the Pacific Ocean.

Several years ago, Mrs. Sanders planted three olive trees in her backyard, without requesting approval from the association. Mistake number one.

Due to oversight and nurturing by Mrs. Sanders, the olive trees grew taller and taller over the next few years. Eventually, they blocked the ocean view of the next-door neighbors, Mr. and Mrs. Merkle. The Merkles complained to the association about the view blockage. The association noticed a disciplinary hearing and requested the Sanders to attend a board of directors meeting to respond to the view obstruction complaint of the Merkles. The Sanders did not attend the hearing because they were busy with other matters. Mistake number two.

The association concluded after the hearing that the Sanders' olive trees blocked the ocean view of the Merkles and, therefore, they must be removed. The Sanders ignored the notice of the ruling from the association. Mistake number three.

Since the olive trees were not removed after notification by the association, the Merkles sent a letter to the Sanders requesting they remove these trees. The Sanders ignored the letter. Mistake number four.

Since the olive trees were not removed after notification by the association and the letter from the Merkles, the Merkles hired attorney Jim Snow to send a demand letter to the Sanders. Mr. Snow's letter threatened the Sanders with litigation if the trees were not removed.

At this point, the Sanders hired me to represent them. I contacted Mr. Snow and requested permission to visit the Merkle property to observe the extent of the view impairment created by the olive trees. Mr. Snow agreed. A site inspection was scheduled. At the site inspection, I could clearly see how the Sanders' olive trees blocked the Pacific Ocean view of the Merkles both from the backyard and from the windows inside the house.

At this point, I conferred privately with the Sanders. I informed them that their trees blocked the Merkles' ocean view and the trees should be removed. I explained that if the trees were not removed, the Merkles, the association, or both would initiate a lawsuit against them, which would result in a court order to remove the trees and assess an award of attorney's fees in favor of the Merkles in excess of $100,000, plus court costs. I also explained that my attorney's fees would cost the Sanders more than $100,000. Thus, there was an exposure to paying attorneys' fees in excess of $300,000, which included my fees, the Merkle's attorney fees, and the association's attorney fees, in addition to the judge ordering the removal of the olive trees.

Dr. Sanders stated that he understood what I said and that he agreed that the olive trees had to be removed. Mrs. Sanders, who had planted and nurtured the trees, and was very proud of them, said, "No. I am not removing the olive trees. Not one branch." Mistake number five.

I was not sure what to do with the husband and wife disagreeing with each other.

When Dr. Sanders walked me to the car, he said, "Barry, you must save my marriage. Those fucking trees are going to destroy my marriage."

After that, I had several subsequent discussions with Mrs. Sanders. Using all the persuasive skills I could muster, I finally convinced Mrs. Sanders to authorize the removal of the trees.

The trees were removed. Mr. Snow sent me a letter stating that the view restoration from removal of the trees was satisfactory and there would be no lawsuit. The association also sent me a letter stating that this matter was satisfactorily resolved.

Dr. and Mrs. Sanders are still happily married but without the three olive trees.

CHAPTER 18

All People Are Equal, But Some Are More Equal Than Others

Sam and Elizabeth Lawrence purchased a single-family residence in a high-end community association in the hills of Montecito, California, just above the city of Santa Barbara. The association consisted of fifteen single-family residences along one street in a gated community. The name of the association was Happy Hills.

The CC&Rs contained an unusual provision stating that the association provided "basic" landscaping for all single-family residences and the common area landscaping surrounding the single-family residences. Part of the ensuing problem was that the CC&Rs did not explain what was meant by "basic" landscaping. The remainder of the problem was that the association engaged in favoritism, legally known as selective or discriminatory enforcement. To be specific, the board members and their friends had very attractive landscaping on their properties and the common area landscaping surrounding their properties. However, the Lawrences noticed that, as the newest owners within the association, i.e., "the new kids on the block," their landscaping was inferior to others' as to both their property and the common area surrounding their property.

When the Lawrences complained to the association about the discriminatory landscaping, the association denied the claim, stating that they had received the same basic landscaping as everyone else.

The Lawrences retained me to represent them. I filed a lawsuit against the association for selective or discriminatory enforcement of the CC&Rs relating to the landscaping.

An interesting thing happened during the two years that the litigation was pending before trial. The association initiated efforts to improve the landscaping on and around the Lawrence property, so that by the time the trial started, the landscaping contrast between the Lawrence property and the other properties were not as dramatic as it had been when I was first retained two years earlier.

The case proceeded to trial before Judge Sterling, who denied the Lawrences' request for a jury trial and their request for a two-month continuance due to chemotherapy that Mr. Lawrence was undergoing at the time. Judge Sterling ruled in favor of the association and against the Lawrences on the basis that their landscaping was "basic" and not unreasonable, as compared to others. Judge Sterling also awarded the association $1,500,000 for attorney's fees and costs, even though Judge Sterling had only requested the attorneys for the association to present the gross amount of the attorney's fees and did not require an itemized statement (date, description of service, and time).

The Lawrences requested me to appeal the decision of Judge Sterling to the California Court of Appeal. Three of the grounds for appeal were: (1) the denial of a jury trial, (2) the denial of the trial continuance request for Mr. Lawrence's cancer treatment, and (3) an improper award for attorney's fees.

At the time of this writing, a decision from the Court of Appeal may be expected in approximately one year.

As George Orwell stated in *Animal Farm*: "All animals are equal, but some are more equal than others." The same rule applies to people. Some people treat other people "more equal" than others.

What do you think the decision of the Court of Appeal will be? The author believes that there are good grounds for an appeal and the Lawrences are likely to prevail.

CHAPTER 19

Is It Possible That No One Is Responsible For Repetitive Water Intrusion Destroying A High-End Luxury Condominium?

John Soltan was the owner and occupant of a high-end luxury condominium in a building consisting of fifteen stories in Santa Monica, California. Mr. Soltan's unit was on the tenth floor, which provided an attractive view of the ocean and the city lights. For the initial ten years of his occupancy, there were no problems. Then, Mr. Soltan noticed repetitive water intrusion from the ceiling every few months. As a result of his investigation, he determined that his upstairs neighbor, Mr. Josh Jordan, was suffering from dementia or Alzheimer's disease, which caused him to leave water running in the kitchen sink and the bathtub. This continuous running water resulted in the flooding of the Jordan unit, as well as the Soltan unit below.

Mr. Soltan complained to Mr. Jordan about the water intrusion. When there was no response from Mr. Jordan, Mr. Soltan complained to Mr. Jordan's children, a son, who is an attorney, and a daughter, who is a psychologist. When these children did not respond, Mr. Soltan complained to his homeowners' association, known as Santa Monica Beach. The association stated that it would investigate, but it did nothing. The association did not cite or fine Mr. Jordan or even request him to attend a disciplinary hearing. Further, the association took no action to discourage the repetitive water intrusion into the Soltan property.

It should be noted that the area between the Jordan floor and the Soltan ceiling is association common area. This is the area through which water passed from the Jordan property into the Soltan property.

At this point, Mr. Soltan retained me to represent him. I filed a lawsuit against Mr. Jordan and the association. Mr. Jordan contended that since he had dementia or Alzheimer's disease, he was not responsible for his actions. The association contended that since it did not cause the water intrusion, it is not responsible for Mr. Soltan's damages.

In its current condition, Mr. Soltan is unable to sell or even refinance his property. To make matters worse, he cannot even remediate the water damage in his property due to the likelihood of yet another water intrusion from the Jordan property.

Is it possible that no one is responsible for the water intrusion repetitively entering the Soltan property? I don't think so.

This case just settled prior to trial for a payment to Mr. Soltan of $200,000. Mr. Jordan paid $190,000 and the association paid $10,000.

CHAPTER 20

Can You Be Sued For Making A Recommendation, Even Though You Do Not Have The Authority To Make A Binding Decision?

Joshua Sloan, an experienced and well-respected architect, was retained by Ocean View Homeowners' Association in Newport Beach to provide recommendations to the architectural committee and the board of directors of the association on an "as-needed" basis.

Since Mr. Sloan was not a member of the architectural committee or the board of directors, Mr. Sloan had no authority to make a binding decision on the part of the association. His role was simply to make an architectural recommendation, when and if requested. With most architectural decisions, the association did not ask Mr. Sloan for a recommendation. A request for a recommendation was generally sought only in complicated or contentious matters.

Mr. and Mrs. Bennett sought architectural approval from the association for a major remodel of their residence. The Bennetts sought to expand and enlarge their residence so that they would increase their view of the Pacific Ocean.

Mr. and Mrs. Elliott were the next-door neighbors to the Bennetts. The Elliotts objected to the Bennetts' proposed remodeling project because it would reduce their own view of the Pacific Ocean. The Bennetts' remodel would increase the Bennett's view of the Pacific Ocean by about 25 percent and decrease the Elliotts' view of the Pacific Ocean also by about 25 percent.

The CC&Rs for the association state that the remodeling of any residence may not "unreasonably interfere" with any other property owner's view of the Pacific Ocean.

Anticipating a lawsuit from either the Elliotts or the Bennetts, the association sought the recommendation of Mr. Sloan. Mr. Sloan recommended that the association reject the Bennetts' architectural application and direct them to submit a revised architectural application that does not decrease the Elliotts' view of the Pacific Ocean to such an extent.

The Bennetts responded by filing a lawsuit in the Orange County Superior Court against the association, the Elliotts, the association's community manager, and Mr. Sloan.

The Bennetts contended in their lawsuit that Mr. Sloan had a conflict of interest because several years previously

Mr. Sloan had been retained by the Elliotts to develop plans for their own home remodeling project, which had been approved by the association, and had resulted in the Pacific Ocean view that was now in jeopardy from the Bennetts' proposed remodeling project. The Bennetts contended that Mr. Sloan should have declined the current assignment by the association based on his previous representation of the Elliotts.

Mr. Sloan retained me to represent him after he received the lawsuit.

I contacted the association and requested the association to represent Mr. Sloan because he had been acting as an "agent" for the association. The association declined, stating that it had no duty to provide representation.

On behalf of Mr. Sloan, I filed an answer to the Bennetts' complaint denying that there was any conflict of interest because Mr. Sloan had never represented the Bennetts and the association knew of Mr. Sloan's prior representation of the Elliotts at the time it voted to reject the Bennett's architectural plans. In addition, I filed a cross-complaint against the association demanding that the association pay Mr. Sloan's attorney's fees for the litigation.

Regrettably, Mr. Sloan did not have liability insurance and he did not have a written employment contract with the association. Thus, Mr. Sloan had to pay his own attorney's fees, while all the other defendants were represented by their liability insurance carriers.

This case was recently settled. As part of the settlement, Mr. Sloan paid $25,000 to the Bennetts to avoid a trial that would probably have cost him an additional $50,000 in attorney's fees and the potential for an adverse judgment in excess of $1,000,000 in favor of the Bennetts.

Do you think this is a fair result for Mr. Sloan? I don't think so.

CHAPTER 21

How Do You Change The Board Of Directors Of A Community Association?

Many people complain about the management and operation of the board of directors of their community association. Beyond simply complaining, how does a property owner cause a change in the board of directors? There are basically two ways to accomplish this change.

The first way concerns the next scheduled election of the board of directors. The property owner can seek to have a new slate of directors elected through the association's normal election process. Sometimes this process is not effective because of the time between elections, the staggered terms of directors, the association's election rules, or incumbent misconduct regarding the election, making it difficult for new persons to join the board of directors.

The second way concerns a recall election. This is the story of a recall election.

There is a twenty-unit residential project in Pasadena with a five-member board of directors, known as Sunrise Homeowners' Association. In an election James Carlson and his wife, Donna Carlson, were elected to the board. Mr. Carlson was elected president. At the same time two others who were supporters of the Carlsons were also elected, thereby creating a four-to-one split on the five-member board of directors.

There were three problems created by the election of the Carlsons to the board of directors.

First, it was discovered after the election that Mr. Carlson had several felony convictions, including for fraud. Second, the association failed to comply with its own election rules relating to the appointment of the inspector of elections or timely notice to the owners regarding the nomination of candidates or the distribution of ballots. Third, the new board declined to share the association's financial information with the members, despite several requests and a statutory obligation to do so. The sole minority board member, Ann Canter, retained me to invalidate the election through a petition to recall the board and elect a new slate of directors.

My first assignment was to prepare a petition to recall the board of directors and elect a new slate of directors to the board of directors. Accordingly, I drafted and served the petition on the board of directors. I expected to be notified of a date for the recall election. However, instead of scheduling the recall election, the board of directors ignored the recall petition and declined to set a date for the recall election, because the board of directors did not want to be recalled.

I then filed a petition for writ of mandate in the Los Angeles County Superior Court in Pasadena asking the judge to order the association to conduct the recall election on a timely basis with the correct procedures. After several months of legal battles, the judge agreed with me and issued the order.

The recall election was conducted, as ordered by the judge. The prior board was removed and the new board was elected. The association has been operating smoothly and efficiently ever since the recall election.

CHAPTER 22

A Property Owner Must Continually Monitor The Architectural Review Process

Ms. Sarah Kell resided in Miramonte Community Association in San Juan Capistrano, California. The Kell home faced property to the north, which was owned by Mr. and Mrs. Jackson. The Jacksons submitted an architectural application to the association to install an outside stairway on the north side of their home, so that their teenage son could access his second-story bedroom without disturbing his parents.

Mr. and Mrs. Jackson sent a copy of the architectural application to Ms. Kell, as required for "neighbor awareness." Since the exterior stairs, as depicted on the application, were to be located on the north side of the Jackson property, Ms. Kell would not see the stairway from her house. Therefore, she did not object to the outside stairway.

At the hearing before the association's architectural committee, the committee decided that the stairway would be more architecturally attractive if it was constructed on the south side of the Jackson property rather than the north side. However, as stated above, the south side of the Jackson property faced the Kell property, whereas the north side did not. The architectural committee approved the outside stairway on the south side of the Jackson property. Ms. Kell did not attend the hearing of the architectural committee and did not receive any notification that the stairway was going to be constructed on the south side of the Jackson property rather than the north side as originally planned.

A few months later, Ms. Kell noticed that the outside stairway was being constructed on the south side rather than the north side of the Jackson property. By the time Ms. Kell sent a letter to the association and to the Jacksons, complaining about the exterior stairway, the stairway construction was completed.

Ms. Kell retained attorney Sam Shephard to represent her in filing a lawsuit against the association and the Jacksons concerning the exterior stairway. Ms. Kell contended that she should have been notified of the change in the plans for the exterior stairway before it was constructed. The association and the Jacksons contended that no subsequent notice was required.

As the lawsuit proceeded to trial, I was retained by attorney Sam Shephard to testify as an expert witness on community association's standards and practices. My testimony was that if there is a significant change to an architectural application by the association's architectural committee, and this case presented a significant change, the association and/or the applicant, the Jacksons, should have provided Ms. Kell with written notice of the change and given her an opportunity to object before it was approved by the architectural committee.

The association retained attorney Stan Stead as its expert, who testified that no subsequent notice was required. He stated that the governing documents of the association required only one notice to neighbors and there was no requirement for any subsequent notice to any neighbor if the architectural committee required changes to the architectural application.

This case proceeded to trial in the Orange County Superior Court before Judge Markham. Judge Markham ruled in favor of the association and the Jacksons and against Ms. Kell. He ruled that no subsequent notice was required to be submitted to Ms. Kell and that Ms. Kell should have attended the architectural committee meeting if she wanted to become aware of the decision or provide input as to the proposed stairway.

The first lesson here is that a property owner must continually monitor proposed architectural changes that might impact him or her. The second lesson is that a judge does not always decide a case the way you might expect.

ACKNOWLEDGMENTS

Almost two years ago, my wife, Myra C. Ross, passed away due to intestinal cancer after forty-three years of marriage. During our marriage, I frequently discussed my pending cases with Myra. Although she was not a lawyer, she often gave me helpful advice as to how I should represent my clients. In addition, she told me that I should write a book about these cases because they are so interesting. I never had time to write a book while we were married. However, I would not have written this book without Myra's inspiration and guidance. Therefore, I dedicate this book to Myra, my wife, best friend, and advisor.

I also want to thank my two proofreaders, who provided substantive suggestions: Karla Jimenez and Debbie Orgen.

Finally, I want to thank my writing coach Henry DeVries of Indie Books International, who provided guidance, encouragement, suggestions, and motivation that enabled me to compile and complete this book.

ABOUT THE AUTHOR

Barry A. Ross, JD, has practiced real estate and community association law for fifty years in California. During his career, Mr. Ross has participated in more than one hundred jury and non-jury trials, more than fifty arbitrations and mediations, and twenty appeals to the California Court of Appeal, including the landmark case of *Cabrera v. Alam* (2011) 197 Cal. App. 4th 1077 involving the applicability of the Strategic Lawsuit Against Public Participation to a community association, as described in Chapter 9.

For most of his career, Mr. Ross has focused on community association law. Mr. Ross primarily represents homeowners and business owners against their community associations. Mr. Ross has published many articles for attorneys and non-attorneys on community association laws. He has been a guest speaker on various community association topics before many different groups of attorneys, including the Orange County Bar Association and the San Diego Bar Association.

Mr. Ross has served as an expert witness on community association practices and procedures to trial attorneys on ten community association court cases.

Mr. Ross received a bachelor of arts in psychology from UCLA in 1970. Mr. Ross received a Juris Doctorate from Loyola University School of Law in Los Angeles in 1973. Mr. Ross was admitted to the California Bar in 1973.